THE
OLYMPIAN GAMES
IN ATHENS, 1896

D1562977

THE OLYMPIAN GAMES IN ATHENS, 1896:

The First Modern Olympics

by Burton Holmes

With Photographs by the Author

GROVE PRESS INC.

New York

First Evergreen Edition 1984
First Printing 1984
ISBN: 0-394-62115-8
Library of Congress Catalog Card Number: 83-49389

Printed in the United States of America

GROVE PRESS, INC.
196 West Houston Street
New York, N.Y. 10014

5   4   3   2

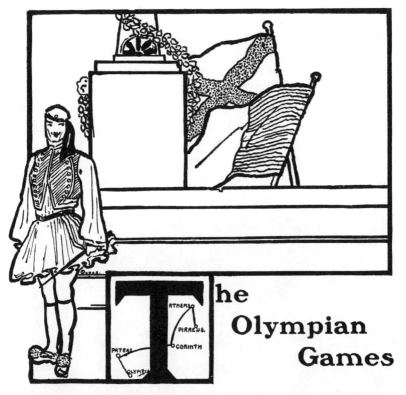

The Olympian Games

IT IS a mistaken belief that he who knows not ancient Greece, as revealed in the immortal works of poetry, philosophy and art, he who has not spent his life in the companionship of the Greek classics, he who cannot in his own soul realize the Greece of old, is not fitted to approach her shores. The Olympian Games were the excuse for my intrusion into the land of the scholar and the archæologist. I knew too well that I would bring to Greece only a love of travel, an eye not wholly blind to beauty, and a deep respect for the history, the letters, and the art of Greece.

While to the student of antiquity Greece offers a larger reward than to any other , for every one she has gifts according to the worth of his mental capacities; and even upon him who, empty-handed, humbly bows before her, she bestows an ample recompense — the power to appreciate and to enjoy her natural charm. Let no one therefore hesitate to visit Greece. Pallas Athene is no longer stern ; she asks of the children of the present century, not that they sacrifice to her upon the altar of unceasing study, but only that they bring to her hearts rightly tuned, eyes alive to form and color, souls in which dwells the love of loveliness. She asks no more than that which almost every one of us can offer.

ON THE ADRIATIC

AN ALBANIAN PORT

Let us, then, without a classical dictionary, without our Homer or our Plato, set forth upon a strictly modern Odyssey.

The shortest way to Greece is from New York to Naples by the Mediterranean route, thence across smiling Italy to Brindisi, and thence in steamers of the Austrian Lloyd to Patras on the western coast of Greece. In nine days we reach Gibraltar, three days later we are in the busy streets of Naples, next night upon the quay of Brindisi, whence we are to cross the Adriatic. And it was with supreme satisfaction that I found myself on the waters of that Adriatic Sea, on which, six years before, I had looked so wistfully from the Venetian towers.

East of Italy I had never been before ; the land which lay before me possessed that charm which ever hovers over the unknown. In the early morning we sight the Albanian coast, then still held by the Turk. For hours we steam south, a wall of barren mountains, grim and cold, upon our left. The land looks desolate and uninhabited, but later our steamer enters a little bay and anchors at a Turkish port, a desolate pile of ruins, near which rise a few new buildings and a custom-house. Albanian shepherds now embark. They introduce us to the Orient. We now feel that our journey has in reality begun. We now for the first time hear Turkish dialects ; while the speech of modern Greece also falls on our ears like a sweet though distorted echo from the past. But

ALBANIANS

we still hear the languages of the Occident — French, Italian, and English. An interesting specimen of Hellenized English may be found in the cabin of the steamer. The rules and regulations are printed in four languages. The following are extracts from the column intended for the edification of English-speaking passengers : " It is prohibited to any

THE ARCHIMANDRITE

passenger to meddle with the command and direction of the vessel, the Captain being the only responsible person." This is not very reassuring, but the awful thought that all the engineers, the sailors, and especially the cooks are irresponsible, is forgotten in our admiration of the elegance of regulation No. 12. It reads, "Passengers having a right to be treated like persons of education will no doubt conform themselves to the rules of good society by respecting their fellow-travelers and by paying a due regard to the fair sex." And then the compiler of this code of ocean ethics concludes by saying to the persons of education above referred to, "Thou shalt not go to bed with thy boots on ! "

Our fellow-passengers are not less interesting. Among them is a prelate of the Greek Church — the Archimandrite of Vienna. A striking contrast of smiling youth and wrinkled age is offered by one charming little Maid of Athens — or some other place — and her grim-faced old nurse ; the

A CONTRAST

two being a contrast analogous to that presented by the bleak Albanian shores upon our left and the smiling hillsides of the Ionian Isles, which, like a necklace of emeralds, seem floating past us on the right. Of our brief stop at lovely Corfu I shall not speak, the charm of the Ionian Islands, visited in leisure two months later, I reserve for another time. Athens is now our destination. We land at Patras, fourteen days after leaving New York. A little railway links Patras to Corinth and Athens with a chain of steel. A more enchanting railway ride than that along the Southern shores of the Corinthian Gulf I have never enjoyed. On one side the mountains of the Peloponnesus, on the other side vineyards stretching down to a gulf

A STATION

whose waters are so blue that artists hesitate to tell the truth
in color, fearing the ridicule of critics who have never sailed
the Grecian seas.   And then beyond the waters, far in the
north, rises that splendid mountain wall whose fame is
immortal, for its watch-towers are named Parnassus and Hel-
icon.   Other names which have thundered down the centuries may be spelled out upon prosaic sign-boards at the
railway stations.   Sicyon is passed, and in a very short

PATRAS

time we hear the blatant shouting of the railway guards :
" Corinthos, twenty-five minutes for luncheon ! — Corinthos.''   Think of it ! — railway sandwiches so near the
site of ancient Corinth !

Our train, however, now rolls on toward Athens, skirting
the shores of the Saronic Gulf and revealing to us glimpses
of the famous islands Ægina and Salamis.   "Does one
travel in Greece on flat cars ? " is the question that may
be suggested by our next experiences.   Although all the

members of our party had first-class tickets, giving us the
right to sit in crowded, stuffy, first-class cars, two of us
resolved that we would not submit to close confinement, and
during a stop at a way-station we climbed into an empty flat
car, and then went trailing along through the glorious spring
morning across the territory of classic Megaris.   Our friends

FIVE MINUTES FOR REFRESHMENTS

look envyingly on us from the tiny windows.   Greek passengers smilingly point out to their companions the two eccen-
tric foreigners on the tail-end of the train.   Meantime we are
enjoying the exhilaration of this flight, and losing nothing of
the scenery which soon becomes imposing.   But as the train
begins its dizzy careening around the Skironian cliffs, a sud-

THE ROYAL PALACE

CAFES IN THE PLACE DE LA CONSTITUTION

den thunder-shower comes rolling over the jagged summits of those rocky heights, the clouds open, tons of water splash down and wash the landscape, and we have the full benefit of this unexpected shower-bath. For fifteen minutes, totally unprotected, we are relentlessly hurled on against a blinding rain. But so brief are these Greek showers and so bright and warm the sunshine which chases them away, that before we reach our destination we are rough-dried, and content in the souvenir of a diverting adventure.

An hour later we arrive in Athens. And as we drive through its modern streets, we are at the same time surprised and disappointed ; surprised to find the handsome shops,

IN MODERN ATHENS

clean pavements, fresh facades ; disappointed to observe that
no reminders of the past are visible and that the inhabitants
are dressed like those of any European city. But the signs
above the shops, at least, are Greek ; and my companions
fresh from college read with the accent of the class-room the
names of tailors, milliners, and jewelers, while here and there

FROM THE HOTEL D'ANGLETERRE

we see displayed in those almost sacred Greek letters the
praises of somebody's pills, of American sewing-machines, or
the announcement of a bargain sale.

At a street corner is a sign in Greek and French, which
tells us that this is the street of Hermes. At the upper end
we see the royal palace, overlooking a large public square ;
our hotel faces the palace, and also overlooks this center of
Athenian life, the Place de la Constitution. Below our

windows are the tables of an open-air café; at the corner is a
kiosk like those in which we buy our daily papers on the
Paris Boulevards.   Coquettish little tram-cars are drawn like
playthings across this square by tiny horses, big enough for
toys.   Beyond we see the balconied façades of the Hotel de

HOTEL DE LA GRANDE BRETAGNE

la Grande Bretagne, while in the distance rises the hill of
Lycabettus, crowned by the little chapel of a hermit.

Great indeed is the distance between yonder hermit's
abode and the café below us ; they are in spirit at least four
hundred years apart.   Bicycles flit through the streets, cabs
and landaus are stationed at the hotel doors.   The public
vehicles are called even to-day "amaxa," the very word, you

BOOTBLACKS

will remember,
Homer used in speaking
of Achilles' chariot.   The
Greek, before he hires one of
these, makes with the charioteer what
is called a "symphony."   Do not mistake my meaning.
The making of a symphony requires no musical talent ; it
demands much firmness of character and a genius for di-
plomacy.   Unless you make a symphony before you start,
there will be a discord when you come to pay your fare.

Imagine a New York hackman as a
party to a "symphony;" there no
doubt would be a "*scherzo*," and
a "*con furore*," and all the move-
ments played "*fortissimo*."

The industry of caring for the
footgear of the Athenian populace
is remarkably developed.   At every
corner, in every square, we find a
line of bootblacks, who, judging

PAPADOPOULOS DRAGOMAN

trom the magnificence of their outfits, must do
a thriving business.   They keep on hand all
kinds of blacking, polish, oils, and dress-
ings, and are prepared to treat every ex-
isting kind of leather from delicate patent-
leather to a piece of Attic beefsteak.   Nor
do we wonder at the importance of
their craft.   For when my friend sits
down to consult his Bædeker, after our
first walk through the streets of Athens,
a young bootblack smiles in triumph at

ALLURING SMILES

the condition of our recently well-polished shoes.   Athenian
dust is the dustiest dust in all the world.   Though it may
be sprinkled into momentary immobility by the municipal
employees, the dust of Athens never gives up the fight.   It
dries and rises in the wake of the sprinkling brigade, mock-
ing the daily efforts to subdue it.   Its vitality convinces us
that it must be the dust of those old Greeks who never
were subdued.   Ere we ruin the luster imparted to our
shoes, we take our places at one of the numerous cafés,
and tell the waiter to bring us whatever may be the favorite
drink of the Athenians.   "Mastica is what you want;" and

GRECIAN PRETZELS

presently he re-
turns with two big
glasses, a carafe
of water, and two
tiny glasses filled
with a clear thin
liquor.   Follow-
ing the example of
the citizens whose
order was like our
own, we empty
the mastica into

the big glass and then pour water slowly in upon it.   This produces a cloudy opalescent mixture, which to our unaccustomed palates suggests weak paregoric.   But a week later I have learned to like mastica and drink of it as freely as the Greeks ; for it is not in any way injurious, and is one of the best preventives of fever known in Greece.   Of course coffee is also in great demand at these cafés ; prepared in Oriental fashion, it is thick, delicious, and far less harmful than coffee as we prepare it.   The grounds lie half an inch deep in the cup after we have finished.   We have sipped only the exquisite savor, the nerve-destroying element has been left undisturbed.   Another luxury to be enjoyed at a Greek "cafenion" is the pistachio-nut.   "Pistikia" are not served by the establishment but peddled by itinerant dealers. The nuts have been roasted, the shells are slightly parted. Opening pistachio-nuts is as fascinating an occupation as cutting the leaves of a new book, and we sit for hours prying apart the tiny shells and devouring the contents ; every now

EVZONOI

GRECIAN SOLDIERS

GREEK SOLDIERS

and then hailing a passing vender to obtain a fresh supply. I think I ate about six thousand nuts while in Greece, and in the purchase of them learned how to bargain with a Greek. Fourteen for ten lepta — about one cent — is the usual rate ; to obtain twenty for the same price requires courage and persistence. Frequently the exasperated Greek offers to gamble with you. He picks up a handful, lays them on the table, and tells you to guess, "odd or even." If you win, he smiles, congratulates you, and going to another table sells pistachio-nuts for five cents apiece to a stranger newly arrived, and thus recoups his losses.

While sipping coffee and cracking pistachio-nuts, we observe the passers-by with interest. The men as a rule are dressed like the average civilized man in any land ; that is, badly dressed, in the most convenient and hideous garb ever devised. The women ape Paris fashions.
the officers are well-groomed, tightly laced, typical continental *militaires*. But the soldiers, at least the Evzonoi, are a delight to the eye, with their bright red fezes, long blue tassels, short embroidered jackets, *fustanellas* of innumerable pleats, and *tsarukia* of red leather with tufts of red upon the tips of the turned-up toes. One of these gorgeous warriors presumed to be amused at sight of the broad-brimmed hat with a puggaree which sheltered me from the ardent Athenian sun. I returned

A MAN AND A PIG

his smile finding the swing of his starched skirt equally mirth-
provoking. My artist friend thereupon makes a little sketch
to illustrate the incident, putting into my mouth the words,
"Well, I don't see that people who dress themselves in
lamp-shades have any call to laugh at my hat!"

Greek currency also will afford the stranger a little amusement and considerable annoyance. The modern Greek
drachma is nominally a franc, twenty cents ; but in the
unfortunate financial condition of the country the drachma
has depreciated. All the gold and silver coin of Greece

The American in Athens.
" Well ! I don't see that people who dress themselves
in lamp-shades have any call to laugh at my hat ! "

A JOKE BY JACOMB-HOOD

has passed out of the
kingdom, and is in
use upon the Conti-
nent. The paper
currency alone re-
mains, a paper drach-
ma being worth only
about twelve cents.
Most of this paper is
as depreciated in
quality as in value,
and unless carefully
handled the ragged

bills will fall to pieces in your fingers. In honor of the
Games, a new issue of bank notes was made. The new
notes come in the form of a long ribbon of fresh, crisp
coupons. The American athletes used to rush into Cook's
office every morning and ask, " How much to-day for a
yard of drachmas ? " And the clerks, consulting the latest
exchange-bulletins, would measure off the Greek " green-
backs " according to the value of the French or English
gold laid on the counter by the delighted purchaser, who
by this operation doubled instantaneously the value of his
pocket-money. But at hotels, patronized by foreigners the

bills are always made out on a gold basis. To pay a bill of a hundred francs requires almost two hundred paper drachma. Only in dealing with unsophisticated Greeks, if such there are, could we gain anything through the cheapness of Greek money. The traveler is always made to pay in francs (gold value) even for such articles or service as will be given to the native for the same number of paper drachmas. It is affirmed that if the Greek cannot get more from the stranger than would satisfy him if paid by a fellow-countryman he will refuse to sell.

Another curious point about Greek money is that there are no bank notes of the denomination of five drachma.

BUYING DRACHMAS BY THE YARD

Accordingly, when one day my friend tendered a ten drachma bill in exchange for a bust of the Olympian Hermes, for which five drachmas had been asked, the youthful art-dealer calmly folded the proffered bill, tore it neatly into two equal parts, pocketed the one and handed back the other. He met our protestations with the explanation that half of ten was five, and that we had therefore received the proper change ; nor had we any difficulty in disposing of the mutilated half-bill. In fact, I never again saw ten drachma bills intact, for before they have been long in circulation they are cut up into fives. Many travelers object because at the big hotels the charges are not made in the money of the country. To which objection the proprietors reply that there are other hotels and restaurants where any kind of money will be welcome, and where Greek accommodations will be given for Greek money. The competition between the native establishments, called Xenodochion, and the pretentious hotels managed on French and Swiss lines is not very keen. I think one reason why so few travelers visit the interior of Greece is that the guide-books tell them that

AN ART DEALER

the Xenodochion of Athens is the type of those which
the pilgrims in the provinces will be compelled to put up
with ; and we can pardon those whose enthusiasm to visit
classic sites does not conquer their aversion to a bill-of-fare
like the one offered by the native cuisine. Don't ask me to
describe it ; the mixture which the Greek chef ladles out to
hungry guests is the most impersonal thing I ever saw.

The modern Greeks, especially in cities, are abandoning
their picturesque but ridiculously complicated costume in
favor of that cheap, ready-made attire which is supposed
to be the badge of civilization. This shoddy modern dress,
invariably ill-fitting, robs them of all dignity, and successfully
conceals whatever of grace and beauty they have inherited
from the Greeks of other days. But if in the streets of

A PUBLIC KITCHEN

Athens we see comparatively few contrasting costumes, the most striking architectural contrasts are not wanting. We find side by side with the commonplace shops and churches of to-day, remnants of medieval Athens in the form of Byzantine churches. One of these stands near the new cathedral. It is called the Small Metropolis, or the church of the Panagia Gorgopiko. Many fine archaic reliefs and ancient

GREEK NATIONAL DRESS

inscriptions have been built into the walls of the tiny church; it is in fact composed of the débris of antiquity. The resulting structure is most quaint and interesting, a sort of curio which ought to be kept safely in a big glass case. It is regrettable that seventy of these little gems of Byzantine architecture have already been torn down to make way for ugly modern structures.

CHURCH OF THE PANAGIA GORGOPIKO

Just outside the doorway of this chapel there lies a large block of gray marble. On it is carved in Greek letters an inscription which, if authentic, and many scholars admit its authority, gives to that stone a priceless value: "This is the stone from Cana of Galilee, where Jesus Christ our Lord turned water into wine." The stone was brought to Athens long ago by pilgrims from the Holy Land.

A BYZANTINE CHURCH

This mingling of the souvenirs of far separated epochs is in many places strikingly apparent. Stately columns reared by Hadrian when Rome was mistress of the world stand like a group of minarets beside an old dilapidated mosque built by the Turk when he was striving after universal sway. Then, looking through the portico of the Moslem builder, we see a modern house erected in the reign of George the First, king of the Greeks of to-day. And, did we care further to prosecute our search, we could find structures built by the

Franks and the Venetians who in turn were masters of the land, and on the slope of the Acropolis, almost within the shadow of the Parthenon, we may find a little group of dwellings so like the whitewashed houses in the native quarter of Algiers that we expect to see at every corner the flowing burnoose of an Arab Kaid.   This is, however, the abode of poverty, the headquarters of the laundresses of Athens.   The

BYZANTINE AND ROMAN RUINS

newly washed linen of the Athenians is hung out to dry upon
the sacred slope of classic Athens. Although old Athens
lodged her gods in temples of immortal grandeur, and her
rich men in splendid palaces, her humble citizens and her
many slaves were miserably provided for. The public life
was everything, the home was but a place to sleep. Even
to-day the poor Athenians make of the public thoroughfare a
workshop, sleeping-room, or restaurant, according to the
hour. At lunch-time many a young Pericles and Alcibiades
may be seen feasting
on bread and jam
upon the public curb ;
and while discoursing
upon sweet things I
must not fail to speak
a word in praise of
the celebrated honey
of Hymettos which is
served us every morn-
ing, and it is indeed
delicious. The clas-
sic bees of Mt. Hy-
mettos, have, it is
said, now emigrated
to another height,
but, perhaps because
the honey is so sticky,
the old name adheres
to it. Another very
curious feature of our
Athenian breakfasts
is the fresh butter,
which at first we do
not dare to taste, but

THE TEMPLE OF THESEUS

which upon acquaintance we soon learn to relish. It is almost pure white, its consistency is that of whipped cream, and sometimes we are obliged, bidding defiance to table etiquette, to dip up and spread the butter with a spoon.

Midnight and midday are in Athens alike in one respect : the streets and squares are deserted at the stroke of twelve, be it by day or night, for at noon as well as at midnight Athens sleeps. It

HAPPY

is said that save foreigners and dogs no one ever ventures out when the sun is high. Athenian humanity, having lunched, apparently ceases to exist until the shadows have grown long again, until the magic light of the early evening has banished all that glaring ugliness which at high noon descends upon the city. For it must be said that modern Athens illuminated by the crude vertical rays of the noon-day sun is positively ugly and repellent. There is practically no shade in Athens proper. There is, however, behind the palace a lovely royal garden where shrubs and flowers and grass and all kinds of fresh green things are shielded from Apollo's burning arrows by masses of rich foliage. Nor is this garden, doubly delicious because it is unique in Athens, reserved for selfish enjoyment by the royal family. Three afternoons in every week the garden gates are thrown open that all Athens

JEALOUS

may for the nonce forget its arid Attic surroundings in the purple gloom of the wistaria arbors. This garden is the most expensive luxury in Greece, for it has been created, as it were, from the Attic desert. Water and vegetable soil are scarcities

AN ATHENIAN HOME

in Athens, and vast sums were spent here by the Bavarian King, Otho, to please his queen Amalie, who longed for shade and verdure which before her time did not exist in Athens.

And as we linger here there naturally rises before us the face of him who rules the destinies of Greece to-day, George

KING GEORGE

the First, King of the Hellenes. He is a Danish Prince, son of the King of Denmark, and brother to Queen Alexandra of England. In 1863, he was called to fill the throne left vacant by King Otho, the unpopular German Prince who had been selected by an International Congress to rule the Greeks, but who, after a reign of about thirty years, was invited to extend indefinitely the vacation which he had unwisely taken. King George, although a man of peace, has endowed Greece with more territory than many a famous conqueror. Some thirty-three years ago he came from his home in the far north bringing to the nation that had itself chosen him as king, a royal gift — the deeds by which Great Britain transferred to the new kingdom the seven beautiful Ionian Islands which

QUEEN OLGA

the English had long before taken from the Turk.   Greece
being delivered from Moslem conquerors, Great Britain grace-
fully returned the islands which by her occupation she had
preserved from ruin.   Queen Olga, consort of King George,
was a Russian princess.   Under the sway of this royal pair
who came to Greece, the southernmost of European
countries, from two lands which lie in the farthest north, the
nation has, in spite of her misfortunes, steadily progressed.

King George at his coronation said, "I wish to make of
Greece the model kingdom of the Orient." This he has in a

IN THE ROYAL GARDEN

TRICOUPIS

certain measure accomplished. The brigands, at one time the scourge of Greece, are now plying their trade on the other side of the Turkish border, and life and property are to-day no safer in Denmark than they are in Greece. Much credit for the progress made by Greece is due to the Prime Minister, Tricoupis, of whom a French writer has said: "He has multiplied the railways and highroads, created and improved the ports of commerce, built light-houses on the dangerous coasts, dressed up the soldiers in new uniforms with brightly polished buttons. He has decreed that the Greek navy shall no longer maneuver on land, and that the Greek cavalry shall not march on foot."

And these good works were much approved of by the people. Shepherds from Arcadia and tillers of

PRINCE CONSTANTINE

IN THE ROYAL GARDEN

the soil from Thessaly looked admiringly on their torpedo-boats and men-of-war, on the brisk regiments of the spick-and-span new army and cried, "Zito, Tricoupis!" But when they were asked to pay for these little luxuries they viewed them in another light. The tide of public favor turned against the man whose life-endeavor was to place Greece in the front rank of nations. The suffrages of a people who expected

PALACE OF THE CROWN PRINCE

him to produce revenues without imposing taxes, drove him into retirement and broke his heart. He died in France, of disappointment, they say, a few days after the Olympian Games had been brought to a triumphant termination.

But we have come to Athens, not to discuss political economy, but to attend the Olympian Festival of 1896.

In April, 1896, Athens invited the world to join in a revival of the Olympian Games which had been the glory and the pride of Ancient Greece. To understand the full significance of this modern festival we should know something of the Olympian Games of antiquity. The old Olympian Festival was never held in Athens. The Attic city had her athletic festivals, the Panathenaic Games, but the great national games were held at Olympia, a sacred place near the western coast of Greece. The site of Olympia had been buried beneath the sands of time until archæologists from Germany uncovered the wreck of its temples, stadia, theaters, and treasure-houses, eloquent reminders of a heroic past. To-day we may travel thither in modern railway cars and look upon the ruins of its temples and the shattered remnants of its mul-   titude of statues.

THE HERMES OF OLYMPIA

A modern hotel caters to the comfort of the traveler, a little museum offers him a feast of beauty.   Supreme among the treasures of the museum of Olympia is the most perfect male figure that has come to us from the artistic past, the Hermes of Praxiteles.   Authorities agree that Olympia was not a city of importance, being rather an assemblage of shrines and temples, a place to which all Greece repaired once in four

HOTEL AND MUSEUM AT OLYMPIA

years to worship the Greek gods and to attend the games here celebrated in honor of Zeus, the deity better known to us as Jupiter Olympus.   Olympia was not the dwelling-place of Zeus ; the father of the gods held his court on the crest of Mt. Olympus far away in Thessaly.   But it was at Olympia that Zeus was honored by the celebration of the games, of which the festival of 1896 is a revival.   The first recorded games, those of 776 B. C., when first the measurement of

time by Olympiads was begun, were but
a revival of still more ancient observ-
ances, the origin of which has been
ascribed to Hercules.

As we look upon the sculptured
gods and men who on the pediment of Olympia's great temple
were actually seen, admired, and
praised by almost every great Greek
who ever lived, our thoughts go back
to those old games, and we long to
see the athletes, the spectators, and
the pilgrims on whom these images of
stone looked down.   Yet these stones
were new when the games were already
a long established institution, for Homer
describes many of the contests which   RESTORATION OF A VICTORY, OLYMPIA
are known to have figured in the Olympian Games.   Some of
these are pictured in the Egyptian wall-paintings which

FROM THE OLYMPIAN TEMPLES

are two thousand years older than the earliest recorded games. The ancient games were exclusively Hellenic in character, to be of pure Greek blood was essential in contestants.

The season for the festival, like the Christian Easter, is dependent upon the moon. The games were held between the new and full moon nearest to the summer solstice, that is, late in June or early in July. The sacred month, or

FROM THE PEDIMENT OF AN OLYMPIAN TEMPLE

Hieromenia, began with the new moon. A truce was then proclaimed throughout the Hellenic world ; warring states withdrew their armies from the field and sent their athletes to meet, in friendly trials of strength, the youth of other states with which they had just been at war, the warriors with whom they would again contend upon the field of blood after the sacred month had closed. No armed men could enter the territory of Elis. Pilgrims to Olympia were protected by the most stringent measures. Those who assaulted them were fined, and, worst of punishments, excluded from the temples, and denied the right of witnessing the games. When the old astronomers had determined the precise date of the festival, the proclamation of the games was made, and heralds of peace were sent to the remotest corners of the Grecian world to announce that the lists were open, to invite all freeborn Greeks to enter for the contests, and, most important of all, to bid those who were at war to desist from the struggle until the great Pan-Hellenic festival in honor of the Father of Gods and Men had been duly celebrated.

THE MUSEUM OF OLYMPIA

THE ACADEMY

THE LIBRARY

One herald traveled northward to the shores of the Black
Sea, another sailed away to Asia Minor and the intervening
islands and thence to Syria and Egypt ; a third was sent into
the West to the people of the Greater Greece, of Sicily and
Gaul and Spain.   From all these lands to which went the
heralds came athletes, pilgrims, and spectators, to throng

ENTRANCE FOR THE PUBLIC

Olympia's courts and theaters, which for four long years had
been deserted save by that marvelous population of marble
statues of which the ancient writers speak in words of glowing
admiration.   Even the mutilated marbles which have come
down to us attest the justice of that admiration.   The treasures of Greece are not of gold or silver ; these she lacks ; her

treasure is of marble. The Olympian Hermes, that master piece of the great epoch of Greek sculpture, is the most precious statue in the world to-day. Every year hundreds of travelers come to Olympia merely to look upon that perfect form. Put all the other discoveries at Olympia in one scale, the Hermes in the other, and it will outweigh them all in the estimation of the cultivated world. And not only were gods honored with statues at Olympia, the victors in the games were likewise carved in statues ; but of that vast sculptured army of Olympian victors few traces now remain. Their deeds, however, are recorded in undying verse, for Pindar

ENTRANCE FOR THE ATHLETES

THE STADIUM

GOING TO THE GAMES

wrote and sang of them. The name of the chief victor was given to the Olympiad or period of four years which ensued.

The feats performed by the Olympianikés of old have been recorded by the story-tellers of antiquity.

One, Milo, was so strong, especially in wrist and hands, that no one could bend or even move his little finger when he held it rigid. Another, Melamcomas, stood during two entire days with arms outstretched. Another, Polydamas, if we are to believe the evidence of tradition, could with one hand arrest the mad career of a four-horse chariot.

THE STADIUM

The old boxing-gloves would make a modern prize-fighter pale with terror. They were of leather, studded copiously with knobs and plates of metal. We are told that the short-distance runners "ran so fast as to be invisible," and this upon a sandy track.

Great honors were the reward of him who conquered in the lists: His native city became famous through his victory; on his return the enthusiastic inhabitants tore down a portion of the city wall that he might not be forced to enter at the gate used by common mortals. Ay, those were glorious days for Greece, those twelve long centuries during which two hundred and ninety-three Olympiads succeeded one another! But these Pagan festivals were destined to be engulfed by the rising tide of Christianity, for in the fourth century after Christ, the Roman Emperor Theodosius, thinking to crush Paganism by abolishing Pagan rites, decreed that

ATHENIAN MULTITUDES

THEIR MAJESTIES OF ENGLAND AND GREECE

no more games should be celebrated in honor of the old Greek
god.   And his mandate held good for fifteen centuries.   During the long dark ages of slavery to Vandal, Venetian, Frank,
or Turk, the Greeks forgot their ancient gods and their ancient
games.   The temples and stadia were destroyed, the marble
deities and athletes slept amid the ruins until a recent yester-
day, when they were brought to light through the enterprise
of foreign archæologists.   But to the Greeks themselves is
due the credit of the revival of the Olympian Games.

Well may the Athenians exclaim, "Ay, it is living Greece
once more!" as they throng into the restored Stadium,
where in the presence of a Christian multitude a Christian
monarch annuls the Imperial decree of fifteen centuries ago
and inaugurates the first Olympiad of modern times.   The
nations of the world have been invited to take part, and gladly
has the invitation been accepted.   The Greeks have performed miracles of generosity and self-denial to insure a
successful issue of this ambitious fête.   The grand old

A FINISH

Stadium, non-existent for long centuries, was restored at the expense of one man, a modern Crœsus—a Greek of Alexandria, whose name, Giorgios Averoff, has been connected with a thousand other works of public use and public charity. The Athenian Stadium was first laid out three hundred and thirty years before the birth of Christ. The spectators of old sat on the grassy slopes of the two long hill-like embankments which faced each other on both sides of the race-course, and were joined at one end by an imposing hemicycle. About five hundred years later, in the days of the Romans, a wealthy citizen, Herodes Atticus, said to the people, "At your next gathering here I promise you a stadium all of marble." And he kept his word.

In 1896 a modern millionaire made a similar promise and fulfilled it. The Stadium was restored according to the ancient plans. To be seen here and there are darker stones from the original structure among the newer blocks, having been found and set up in

"GET SET!"

places which they occupied fifteen centuries before. The thirty-three aisles and stairways of the Stadium, the 60,000 seats would be familiar to many an Athenian of the second century; but the 60,000 people who to-day occupy the seats would puzzle him, indeed; for among them he would see many "barbarians" from lands undreamed of in his day. The old Athenian spectators whitened or enriched with bright colors the marble sides of the Stadium; we moderns blacken it with our hideous funereal garb. But, in spite of all, the sight is one which thrills us, one the like of which has never before been witnessed in our modern age. The first glimpse of the crowded Stadium is to be numbered among the great sensations of a life time. The impressiveness which attaches to every aggregation of humanity is heightened by a close massing of the people and by the classic outlines of the Stadium.

THE BOSTON TEAM

THE PRINCETON TEAM

ATHLETES IN ACTION

Past the entrance to this now modern course runs the road from Marathon; the Bay of Salamis may be seen from the higher tiers, the Acropolis is visible from nearly every seat. It was this immortal background that gave the modern Olympian Games a deeper, wider significance than has ever dignified any other athletic meeting whatsoever.

For it must be confessed that the chief interest of the Olympian Games of 1896 lay in the splendid setting given them, rather than in the games themselves. From the standpoint of modern athletics the contests witnessed by the imposing audience were not remarkable save in one respect, the invincibility of our American champions. No records were broken, in fact our men were not called upon even to equal their own best previous work in their respective lines.

The spectators being assembled to the number of 60,000, all waits on the arrival of the Royal party. At the appointed hour, with democratic punctuality, King George, escorted by the committees, makes his entry. With him are the Queen, the Crown-Prince Constantine, and Prince George, the second son. To the music of the Greek National Hymn the little procession traverses the Stadium, while the multitudes stand with heads respectfully uncovered. And mingled with the respect there is a sense of gratitude ; for had it not been for the unselfish and enthusiastic support of the King and Princes, this splendid spectacle would never have been possible. The Crown-Prince as President of the special Greek Committee was no mere figurehead ; he, aided by Prince George, performed much of the work of organization, while without the moral support and sympathy of the Royal Family the successful issue of the festival would have been in doubt.

The opening ceremonies over, let us take up the program for the first day's sports.

The first event is the one-hundred-meter race. This event is considered now, as in ancient times, the most important of those occurring within the limits of the Stadium. Three heats are run. We listen for the victors' names, expecting in the natural order of things to hear the heralds call out such Greek appella- ROBERT GARRETT tions as "Belokas," or "Lagouda-kis !" But no ! The winning names announced have a familiar

BUYING TICKETS FOR THE GAMES

sound, for they are "Curtis," "Lane," and "Burke!"
Not a bad start for us, indeed.

Our little group of spectators from across the sea hugs
itself in joy ; there are distant echoes of college yells, rising
here and there from little groups, and "B. A. A.," and
"Rah, rah, rah!" and for the moment the word "*Amerikis*" is on the lips of all.

And thus it is in nearly all the subsequent events. Nine
times in ten it is the Stars and Stripes that is run up to indi-
cate the winner's nationality. Our country's flag and honor
are upheld by four men from Princeton, and by a team of
athletes who come to the Athens of the Old World from the
Athens of the New, for they wear the colors of the Boston
Athletic Association. There were, of course, contestants
from other nations, and many ambitious Greeks made brave
attempts to prove themselves deserving sons of an immortal
race. But fortune did not favor them. Athletic sports had
not been practiced here on classic soil for many generations,
and the modern Greeks found themselves outclassed in games
which were to them unfamiliar if not totally unknown.

The triple jump is now contested. " What, again ? " we ask ourselves, as Conolly, of Boston, with a victorious hop, skip, and jump, covers forty-five good feet of classic soil,—enough, more than enough to prove that once more we have triumphed ; and a moment later up goes the banner announcing the first victory of the new Olympiad in the "finals ; " and it is the familiar red, white, and blue of the Star Spangled banner that lights up the Grecian sky.

And then the discus-throwing is announced. For this, the most truly Greek of all the contests, no American had originally been entered. The discus is familiar to us only in connection with statues of old athletes in our art-museums.

THE ASSEMBLING MULTITUDE

Our men can put the shot or throw the hammer, but not one of them has ever seen a discus, much less tried to hurl one. The Greeks, upon the other hand, have long been practicing their antique game, and one of their number has acquired a remarkable proficiency, equaling the best recorded throws of old Olympian victors. Nor was he less beautiful of form or graceful of gesture than the model who served as inspiration for the sculptor Myron, hundreds of years ago. Those who watched him in practice affirmed that in the grace of his poses and gestures and in the accuracy of his delivery he could not have been surpassed by the famous statue itself had it come to life. Remembering this we are not surprised at the hesitation of one of our boys, a member of the Princeton team, when requested at the last moment to enter the lists and, all unprepared, meet the Greek champion in an unfamiliar game. But although he hesitated, he did not decline the challenge. With the same undaunted spirit which has ever characterized the Anglo-Saxon race, Robert Garrett, of the Princeton team, took up a

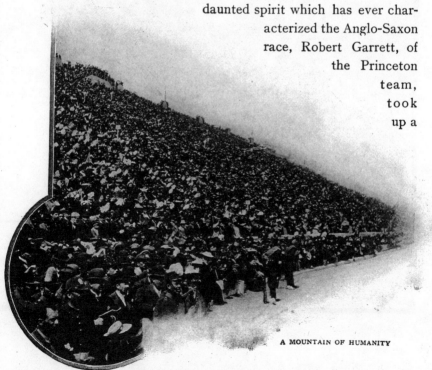

A MOUNTAIN OF HUMANITY

discus for the first time in his life, and stood before the thronging thousands ready to do at least his best for the honor of the Orange and Black and the Stars and Stripes. Our chance of victory seems ridiculously small ; we can but hope that our defeat will not call down the laughter of the Greeks.

The first efforts are merely tentative on the part of our champion. Then with that infinite capacity for "catching on," which seems to be the birthright of every Yankee, Garrett improves, and in his final throw wins more than he or his friends dared to hope for : the right to retire grace-fully and without ridicule. Then Gouskos, the Greek, cer-tain of victory, comes forward. With classic gestures he picks up his discus, and with the grace of an animated antique statue launches it into space. His final throw is marvelously artistic, the heavy discus soars away, descends — then drops. Scarcely has it touched the ground ere all the Stadium is on foot, shouting and waving hats and flags. De-lirious with

THIRTY THOUSAND PEOPLE

delight, Greek gentlemen embrace each other.   For the first time the victory seems theirs, and we may readily imagine their great joy — and then their bitter disappointment, almost despair, when instead of the Greek flag the Stars and Stripes is again hoisted to the victors' mast !   In their enthusiastic admiration for the grace and beauty of their champion's delivery the Greeks had failed to note the very important fact that Garrett's discus, although launched by an unpracticed hand, had touched the earth just seven and one-half inches beyond that which the Greek had so artistically thrown !

All were stupefied.   The Greeks had been defeated at their own classic exercise.   They were overwhelmed by the superior skill and daring of the Americans, to whom they ascribed a supernatural invincibility enabling them to dispense with training and to win at games which they had

never before seen.

To omit further details, the Americans in five contests the first day won the only two decided, took all the heats in two of the others ; and, in spite of the fact that not one of our boys was entered for the fifth event, I verily believe the Greeks expected us to win it.

The second day our flag went up three times.   Our boys are now called the

THE MOUND OF MARATHON

"American invincibles." Garrett at putting the shot sur-
passes the Greek contestant, whose physical perfection was
such that his fellow-countrymen, who still have an eye for
beauty, saluted him as "Hermes."

A Britisher and a Dane then prove their superiority in
lifting weights ; but everything else is ours save one event,
the fifteen-hundred-meter race ; and even this is credited to
us, for although won by a splendid fellow from Australia, it
is put down as an American victory. The Greeks are not
strong in antipodal geography, and when we explain that
Flack, the winner, is an Australian, not an American, they
answer, "Oh, well, that is about the same thing ; we con-
gratulate you."

And the congratulations are sincere, for the Americans are
not begrudged their victories. This is because we are like
those people alluded to by Homer as "the blameless Ethi-
opians" who live so far away as to excite no jealousy.

The third day is devoted to shooting matches in the fine
new shooting-stand on the Phaleric plain. The fourth day
witnesses the gymnastic exercises in the amphitheater, and

is chiefly notable because on that day for the first time the blue and white flag is unfurled in token of a native victory. It is not a heroic one, however, for the Greek, Metrapolous, has proved only   that he can twist and turn on   the flying

THE CREST OF "DEAD-HEAD HILL."

rings more gracefully than the sturdy Germans who excel in almost every one of the other contests.

One Athenian daily paper explained the superiority of the Americans on the ground that they joined to the inherited athletic training of the Anglo-Saxon, the wild impetuosity of the red-skinned Indians! Another, having observed the use of chewing-gum, informed an eager public that the Americans had great endurance because they chewed pitch to strengthen the lungs! Still another expressed great admiration for the piety of the American contestants, for noting but not understanding the custom of blowing on the hands to moisten them before grasping a vaulting-pole or a hammer, the reporter wrote that before each event the Americans bowed their heads in their hands and murmured a brief prayer !

The fifth day is the day of the great race from Marathon. On this event the Greeks founded all their hopes. "If we but win the prize for Marathon, we shall forget all our defeats," was the cry which went up from the vast Hellenic majority of the audience which on Friday fills the Stadium, I had almost said to suffocation. On the surrounding walls, on the hill which dominates the Stadium, on the banks of the Ilyssos, in the gardens of the Zappion, on the boulevards, are massed the thousands who could not force their way into the amphitheater. Never has such a sight been witnessed since the days of antique Athens. The other quarters of the city are deserted, the entire population is massed around and in the Stadium. As early as two o'clock there is not a vacant place, not even on "dead-head hill" which rises high above the marble seats. Still the crowds arrive. On each side rises a huge mountain-range of faces, and all these faces are aglow with expectation and

DEAD HEAD HILL

impatience, all save the four calm marble visages which mark the curve of the course near the royal platform. Why should this scene impress them? They, at least, have witnessed more imposing spectacles, for they stood here during the long centuries of Athenian greatness. They have beheld the splendid Panatheniac gatherings of long ago, they have seen face to face the immortal men whose deeds and songs will never be forgotten. Could they give expression to their thoughts, they would only smile derisively at this throng of moderns, and ask that those who dragged them from their hiding-places deep in the classic earth should bury them again that they might slumber on with the remains of that antiquity of which they formed a part. "We are not of your world," they would say, "let us return a second time into our graves."

I must begin the record of the fifth day with the statement that while the runners are preparing for the start from

READY TO START FROM MARATHON

Marathon, twenty-five miles away, other athletes are contending in the presence of a hundred thousand people. In the Stadium the Americans again cover themselves with glory. Burke wins the finals in the hundred-meter race. Clarke wins the high jump. Curtis flies to victory over the hurdles. Hoyt and Tyler contest the prize for pole-vaulting with the bar one

PREMIER DELAYNNIS

and one-half feet above where it had been abandoned by their Greek opponents. Invincibility is still with the Americans. The Greeks begin to tremble at the thought that our Blake is even now running against their champions on the road from Marathon. When M. Delyannis, the prime minister, saw the American flag go up for the fourth time, he turned to our minister and asked despairingly, "Why did Columbus ever discover your unconquerable country?"

Meantime we must not forget the events transpiring far away on the Marathon road. There Greeks and barbarians are running with grim determination. They know that he who wins the race from Marathon will gain more than

LOUËS, MARATHON VICTOR 1896

ephemeral honor; that the story of his victory will be recited to admiring generations long after the other contestants have passed into oblivion. At Athens the high jump is in progress when mounted couriers arrive announcing that at the sixth mile the Frenchman leads, that the Australian is close behind, that our own gallant Blake is next and doing well.

The spectators are all a-tremble with excitement. They remain on tiptoe as if eager for the first glimpse of the runners who are still eighteen miles away. The Princes make their way to the entrance to await the victor who must soon arrive. The excitement is intense. The suspense is almost painful. All eyes are gazing westward, when at last a cannon-shot is heard. It means that the first runner has reached the outer boulevards, that in a moment he will be here. Who or what he is no one can tell until the crowd outside thunders its joy in a great roar, "A Greek! It is a Greek! Zito, Louës!" And a young Greek peasant, Spiridione Louës, all dust and perspiration, staggers into the Stadium, where a hundred thousand people acclaim him as the hero of the hour.

Then, while from the sloping sides of the Stadium avalanches of applause come crashing down; while the King of Greece so far forgets his royal dignity as to rip the visor from his royal cap in waving it like mad; while staid and proper citizens embrace each other frantically; while tears of joy are shed; while doves, to which long white ribbons are attached, are loosed and flutter in the air; while all Athens utters a triumphant shout, Louës, the simple peasant, the farmer

SHERRING OF CANADA, FIRST

SVANBERG OF SWEDEN, SECOND

FRANK OF AMERICA, THIRD

MARATHON VICTORS IN 1906

from the little hamlet Amarousi, is escorted by two Princes and a Russian Grand Duke — all three embracing, even kissing him — from the entrance to the far end of the Stadium where he is greeted by a royal hand in the midst of such a scene as Athens has not witnessed in a thousand years. All the other runners who arrive in quick succession are, with one exception, Greeks. The native cup of happiness is full. The innate endurance of the Greek peasants prevailed in the great test, over the scientific training of the "American Invincibles." The winner's time, as announced by the judges, was two hours and fifty-eight minutes, the distance forty kilometers, a trifle over twenty-five miles.

The following Tuesday was appointed for the ceremony of the presentation of prizes ; but the ceremony was post-

IN HONOR OF JUPITER PLUVIUS

poned because, the games in his honor being ended, Jupiter
Olympus suddenly abdicated, and the reign of Jupiter Pluvius
began.   Yet in spite of the accession of this unpopular monarch, forty thousand people assembled in the Stadium.
Louës, of Marathon fame, arrives, dressed in the national
costume.   He carries one of the forty thousand umbrellas
displayed about the course, and a bouquet presented by
admiring feminine spectators.   Like a true hero, he is apparently unaffected by his victory, yet enough has already been
done to spoil him.   Immediately after the race he was overwhelmed with favors.   A lady detached her watch and gave it
to him ; a pretty girl placed a be-ribboned dove in his hands ;
a barber enthusiastically declared that Louës's chin should
enjoy a daily scrape at his establishment as long as Louës

SPECTATORS FROM THE U. S. A.

lived and did not grow a beard ; a hatter vowed to hat him ; a
shoemaker swore to shoe him all his days ; a haberdasher
took his oath that he should never lack for underwear and
hosiery ; free meals for life, free drinks, free theater-tickets,
were assured him until his dying day. A rich man gave him
land in his native village, and a wealthy lady offered him the
choice of a large sum of money or a kiss. And Louës, with

CHEZ MME. BAKMETIEFF

a spirit of an amateur, refused the lucre, and with the gal-
lantry of an Olympianiké accepted the other proposition. All
these things he received in addition to the regular prizes, the
presentation of which is now postponed until a fairer day.

And while awaiting clearer skies let me recall a few of the
social diversions that marked the stay of the foreign athletes
in Athens. Numberless entertainments were given in honor
of those who contended in the games. The King gave a

AMERICAN SWIMMERS

HIGH DIVING AT
PHALERON

LOOKING ON

luncheon ; the mayor followed with a picnic ; ambassadors and wealthy citizens all did their share.   Much amusement was caused at the King's luncheon when his majesty sent his chamberlain to the American table with a request that our boys should kindly repeat their strange "war cries."   "The king," he said, "had listened at a distance to these incomprehensible shouts, and was curious to give them a critical

THE AMERICAN TEAM IN 1906

hearing at close quarters."   All arose and gave a rousing, "Rah, rah, rah — Ellas. Ellas, Ellas, Zito !   Hurrah for Greece !" and his majesty expressed himself as satisfied. The papers alluded to these war cries as "Onomatopeia," considering them frenetic shouts difficult to comprehend.

Next to the royal banquet the most enjoyable social event was a picnic given by the charming American wife of the Russian Secretary of Legation, who entertained the Royal Princes and the athletes in the grove of Daphne.

Rather democratic, is it not, to see Prince Constantine, Prince George, and Prince Nicholas of Greece, grouped there with the peasant Louës, and our young Bostonians and Princeton men ?   Prince George, the big fellow seated in the center of the last row, was a prime favorite with all.   As an athlete he could have taken many prizes had he contended. During the weight-lifting match he picked up and noncha- lantly handed to a contestant a dumb-bell, which the latter

TAKING THE HURDLES

could barely lift.   At the picnic he assured one of our men, good humoredly, "I could wrestle with you, and sit on you, too."   Nor was the Crown-Prince a stickler for ceremony. During the games he was ever in the arena, and it was no unusual thing to see him carrying a glass of cognac to a resting athlete, or holding the sweater of another while a contest was in progress.   Even the King himself was not above a little dignified familiarity and amusement upon proper occasions.

KING GEORGE BESTOWS THE OLIVE BRANCH UPON TOM BURKE

"You may win this time," he said to Burke, "but we will beat you in 1900, if I have to run myself!" And the King's words were enshrined in the hearts of every young Greek, if we are to judge from the enthusiasm with which the training for 1900 was undertaken. The open-air gymnasia were thronged every day with school-boys and young men, all striving to emulate the deeds of the Americans.

But sometimes, during the games of 1896, imitation rather than emulation was indulged in. This was apparent, especially in the pistol-shooting matches. The American marks-

TOM BURKE OF BOSTON

men, the Payne brothers, arrived on the very day of the matches, and, to steady their travel-disturbed nerves, took frequent sips of whisky from pocket-flasks. On the second day not a Greek contestant sighted a gun, without first applying a black bottle to his lips. The Messrs. Payne also found it necessary to cover their pistol barrels by smoking with burning matches; the sunlight glistening from the polished steel would have prevented accurate aim. Next day, although the sun was overcast, the Greeks smoked their weapons lock, stock, and barrel, almost reducing them to

ARCHIE HAHN OF MILWAUKEE, WINNER OF THE HUNDRED METERS IN 1906

ashes in their desire to do the proper thing. Thus the flattery of imitation was carried to ludicrous extremes.

But let us now return to the Stadium to witness the closing ceremonies of the games. Below, grouped at the foot of the royal platform, are the various committees, the victorious athletes, the herald Hadji Petros, the Royal Princes, and one victor of whom we have not spoken, the winner of the prize

ARCHIE HAHN WINNING THE HUNDRED METERS, 1906

for the composition of the best ode in Ancient Greek. It is an Englishman from Oxford University who has proved that he can write a better ode in ancient Greek than any of the descendants of the poet Pindar who sang the fame of the Olympianikés in the days of old.

The herald, taking up the list of victors, cries in modern Greek: "Amerikis, Burke. Dromos ekaton-metron," and fifteen centuries look down on the slight, graceful figure of the youth who, mounting to the royal platform, receives from the hand of the King of Greece the first Olympian olive

GYMNASTIC EXERCISES BY ATHENIAN SCHOOLBOYS

branch ever bestowed since that far-off day in the year of our Lord 394, when the last of the old Olympiads was solemnly inaugurated in the land of Elis. The name of the winner of the one-hundred-meter race was always given to the quadrennial period following the games. Therefore the last four years of the nineteenth century must be known to history as the " Olympiad of Thomas Burke, of Boston " !

It must have been a thrilling moment for him as he stood there face to face with the King, the Crown-Prince, and a host of royal personages, while on every side there arose tier on tier of eager faces, a cloud of witnesses which seemed to touch the sky — that same blue sky of Greece which has looked down upon so many heroes.

But again the herald's voice is heard " Dromos tetrakosioi-metron," and the prizes for the four-hundred-meter race are thrust into the already well-filled arms of Burke, who, with his double set of trophies, bows himself from the royal

ATHENIAN MULTITUDES

ATHENIAN SCHOOLBOYS ENTERING THE STADIUM

PROCESSION OF VICTORS

presence and reaching the arena receives congratulations of a
hundred friends. What are the prizes? First, the diplomas
contained in large pasteboard rolls, trimmed with gold paper;
next, a silver medal, on which is stamped a splendid head of
Zeus, and the classic outlines of the Acropolis and of the Parthenon; last and most important, the priceless branch of
olive from the sacred groves of far-away Olympia, a prize
purposely valueless that it may thereby be invaluable. These
are the official prizes, but they are not the only ones, nor
even the first, for during the preceding days the people had

LOUĔS LEADING THE PROCESSION OF VICTORS

made their spontaneous offerings.   One day a ragged bank-
note, worth about sixty cents, was thrust into Burke's hands;
another day a set of postage-stamps was given him by a small
boy, and never could our athletes enter a public cab or car-
riage without creating a good-natured turmoil among the
passers-by, who each and every one claimed the right as
Greeks and hosts to pay the driver of the triumphal chariot.
The other athletes having received their prizes and diplomas,

OLD ATHENS

the victors, according to an ancient custom, march several
times around the vast arena.   The long parade is headed by
the hero of the run from Marathon, resplendent in his gorgeous Greek attire.   He holds aloft the flag of modern Greece
and waves it in response to thunders of applause.   Happy
indeed should be the lives of all these victors if the poet's
words be true, for Pindar, who wrote many odes honoring those
who bore off the highest prizes in olden games, informs us : —

"That he who overcometh hath because of the Games a sweet tranquillity throughout his life forevermore."

As they file past, bearing their prizes in the shadow of the cheering multitude, you may ask who are these unknown thousands massed above us? Are they Greeks, or do they come from foreign lands? It is admitted that the vast majority of these spectators were citizens of Athens; almost the entire population (for Athens boasts only about 130,000 people) was present at the games. The poorest could afford to come, for prices ranged from 12 to 25 cents, according to the proximity of the sections to the royal seats. Strangers there were, but in comparatively meager numbers. The festival itself was purely Hellenic, although so many of the victors were "barbarians."

A few days after the close of that successful celebration, Athens resumes her

THEATER OF DIONYSOS

accustomed air of dignity and calm, and we who do not
follow in the train of the departing crowds become more
keenly conscious of the attraction of that magnet which for
centuries has drawn men to Athens, that rock which is the
eternal glory of Athens—the Acropolis.   The old Greeks
set upon that rock a crown of beauty.   It is there to-day,
magnificent in its mutilation.

Greece was the earliest home of the beautiful, and her
structures and her statues are still the most beautiful, nearer
to perfection than any that have been reared or carved since

WHERE THE AGES SIT AS SPECTATORS

the Parthenon was new.   It is difficult at first to believe this,
yet those whose lives have been devoted to the study of the
arts tell us that it is true ; that when in the mind's eye these
ruined monuments are reconstructed, when the fragments of
Greek statues have been imagined into an unbroken whole,
they will rise before us in absolute perfection, defying modern
art and architecture.   At the base of the rock is the theater
of the wine god, Dionysos ; above looms the wall of the
Acropolis, a wall suggestive of a fortress, for in fact the
Acropolis was first a fortress then a sanctuary.

   To describe properly the various features of this height, to
tell of their significance, must be the task of one much better
versed in history and art than I.   I shall but speak of a visit
to the summit of the sacred hill, and say a word of the buildings which helped to make the fame of Athens.

THE TEMPLE OF WINGED VICTORY

CICERONE

Our cicerone endeavors to make our visit doubly interesting for us by pointing out two things at once, describing one in mongrel French, the other in a sort of Volapuk, composed of the elements of many languages. In the Propylea guides lie in wait for visitors. It is well worth while to listen for an hour to one of these guides on the Acropolis, not for the accurate information to be extracted from them, but for the many new side-lights which their genius throws on history and art. What could be more original than the distinction drawn between Ionic and Doric columns by one guide, who said : " Now, see, old Athens people, all same Ionic people, very luxury people ; when they go fight always wear fine hat, fine shoes. Now, see, Ionic column like peo-

DORIC PILLARS OF THE PROPYLEA

ple who make him;" and, pointing to the graceful capital of one of the Ionic pillars of the little Temple of Victory, he goes on: "See on top the fine hat!": then pointing to the base, "See the fine shoes! Now, Spartan people all same Doric people, very plain people. When they go fight, no hat, no shoes. Now see, Doric column no got a capital, no got a base, all plain like Doric people." After listening to this succinct statement, who could ever mistake an Ionic for a Doric column?

Meantime we have observed with some surprise stains of reddish brown upon the classic columns. Why is it that so many travelers speak of the dazzling whiteness of these walls and pillars of Pentelic marble? They are not white. I quote a recognized authority when I say that they have been toned by centuries of Attic dust to that rich, gold-brown which has turned the Parthenon from marble almost to ruddy gold.

Yes, the Parthenon stands to-day as a ruin, all in white and gold; the whiteness typical of its extreme old age, while the gilded pillars suggest that Nature, conscious of the

THE PROPYLEA

priceless value of this architectural treasure, had resolved to
preserve it by covering its columns with protecting lacquer of
pure gold.

But ruin glares down upon us from every angle of the
noble pile. Time and decay have done their little, and war
and man's thoughtlessness have done the rest. Only two
hundred and fifty years ago the Parthenon was practically

THE WRECK OF AGES

intact. The Turks were masters then in Greece ; a Turkish
garrison occupied the Acropolis ; the Erectheum was a
seraglio ; the Parthenon, after having served as a mosque,
had been converted into a powder magazine. Venice, in
1687, sent her armies to dislodge the infidels. A shell from
the Venetian batteries upon a neighboring hill, found its way,
like a messenger of destruction into the former temple of

PILLARS OF THE PARTHENON BY NIGHT

Athena, and with a roar, which still echoes in the hearts of
all who love the beautiful, the Parthenon, after delighting
the souls of men for 2300 years, became a ruin.   Yet what a
ruin is there ! — more perfect, despite its mutilations than
the proudest structures of the modern world.

The Acropolis, however, owed much of its splendor to an
early disaster.   During the second invasion of the Persians,
four hundred and eighty years before Christ, the Athenians
returning to their beloved city, which had at last been delivered from the Asiatic barbarians as a result of the battle of
Salamis, beheld a spectacle which stirred them to indignation
and to grief.   Their proud old rock still loomed above the
city but, alas, how changed ! Its splendid temples were

THE PARTHENON, WEST FRONT

burned, their walls and columns were cracked and defaced, the precious offerings all were gone, and, worst of all, the marble population of the sacred hill had not escaped the fury of the Asiatic host. The statues of Athena, of the gods and goddesses who had so long been worshiped here, had been tumbled from their pedestals, their members shattered by the fall, their faces marred by vandal hands. The arms, the legs, the hands, the dainty fingers, the noses and the ears of innumerable divinities were scattered here as if an avalanche had swept across the sacred height. We do not wonder that the Athenians wept at sight of all that ruin. But then with an indomitable energy the people of Attica resolved to make a New Athens which should surpass the old whose loss they mourned. And first of all, that this determination to begin from the beginning should be plainly understood, they buried all those muti-   lated deities in

PILLARS OF THE PARTHENON

this consecrated ground, just as the soldiers slain in battle had been buried under the mound at Marathon. And then, at the command of Pericles, two men, Ictinus and Callicrates, whose fame will be immortal, conceived and constructed the most perfect buildings that the world has ever known and Phidias adorned them with his immortal sculptures.

Meantime the entombed gods and goddesses slept on, new statues were reared, the Acropolis became the wonder and the admiration of the ancient world. The entombed gods were worshiped, but in other bodies, for their resting-places had been long forgotten. The centuries roll on and the cult of the Olympic Deities becomes a dead religion. It is well that the sleeping goddesses know not that the Greeks have totally forsaken them. It is well that their sleep shall last until the world, which has long scoffed at their ruined shrines, should have learned to worship that perfect art which was but the expression of Greek religious thought.

It was not until 1886 that the fates were satisfied that the world was ready to render homage before the divinities which the old Persians had cast down. The modern king of Hellenes was strolling here, watching the excavators at their work. Suddenly one of the men shouts from a trench:

THE ACROPOLIS FROM THE THESEON

CARYATIDS OF THE ERECHTHEUM

"Majesty, we have found the gods!" And King George looked and beheld the awakening smiles of fourteen resuscitated goddesses, who, after a sleep of 2300 years, were awakened like sleeping princesses from a magic spell, and saw again the soft light of the Athenian sky.

It was a revelation of a new antiquity ; of an unknown art with a strange exotic charm. Of the gorgeous tinting of these statues, traces remain, but so delicate are these traces that it appears as if the powdery pigments could be dusted off with a feather. The thought that these are the creatures of an epoch not only far removed from our own, but even separated by a wide gulf of time from that of classic Greece gives them a fascination difficult to define. They seem to have come to us, not out of the past of this world, but from another, a pre-existent sphere.

THE ERECHTHEUM

But other fair women of a later epoch grace the ruins of the Acropolis. Beneath the Portico of the Maidens stand those tireless beauties, the Caryatids, who for more than two thousand years have borne all uncomplainingly their heavy burden. They have witnessed here the sacrilege and devastation of the Turk; they saw with horror the pillars

A FALLEN COLUMN

of the Parthenon cast down; but bravely have they stood unshaken by any terrors, worthy daughters of a mighty race.

An Athenian journalist of to-day has compared the Greek people to a Caryatid, upon whose head fate has amused herself by piling up a weight of discouragements and misfortunes. If we look back into her history, we shall

THE PARTHENON

see that Greece has borne up beneath the burden of the Romans, Goths, and Ostrogoths, of the Vandals and the Slavs, of the Franks, the Catalans, and the Venetians, and — for the list is not yet finished — of the Florentines, the Genoese, and for nearly four hundred years she has all but succumbed beneath the barbarous oppression of the Turk.

But the traveler need not be deeply versed in history nor in art to feel the charm that with the evening descends upon the sacred height of the Acropolis. The time-stained pillars of the Parthenon are bathed in an atmosphere of rosy glory, the fluted columns reflect the sunset fires once again as they have done unnumbered times before. No ; not unnumbered; for we know the date of their erection,

ARCHAIC GODDESSES

THE PORTICO OF THE MAIDENS

TEMPLE OF THESEUS

and by a simple reckoning we learn that they have stood here for about nine hundred thousand days — that nearly a million sunsets have gilded these immortal marbles. And see how the glory seems to hover over Salamis and that narrow strait where was fought the greatest naval battle of antiquity! There the Athenians and their allies, under the gallant leader Themistocles, routed the Persian fleets of Xerxes, and saved not only the civilization of the Greeks, but of the world.

AN ATHENIAN VISTA

But if at sunset the Acropolis enchants us, moonlight amid the ruins brings a new inspiration and makes of those who linger there mute poets who feel within themselves a thousand cantos and strive vainly to give forth in words the thoughts that crowd upon them. But since Byron sang, no poet has found voice to utter all that these immortal marbles whisper to him. We are reduced, then. to mute wonder and admiration for the magnificent creations of those old Greeks, which after more than two thousand years of the world's progress are still the nearest to perfection.

The Greeks of classic times soared higher than the greatest of our moderns in philosophic thought, in poetry, in the drama, in architecture, and in art. All that is best in us has been bequeathed to us by them. Let us, then, ere we bid farewell to Athens, freely and gratefully acknowledge our infinite indebtedness to Greece !

HERMES